Green Parrots in my Garden

Poems from the Arab Middle East

JANE ROSS, PhD

BAYEUX ARTS
DIGITAL-TRADITIONAL PUBLISHING

Green Parrots in my Garden *Poems from the Arab Middle East*

Manufactured in Canada
Copyright © 2021 Jane Ross
Published in Canada by BAYEUX ARTS, INC.
2403, 310-6th Avenue, S.E. Calgary, Canada T2G 1L7
Print and binding by Friesens, Manitoba.

CONCEPTS, RESEARCH, DESIGN: Jane Ross. InDesign: Jessica Ryan
Cover image: from an artifactual tin tray with hand-painted image
by the kindness of Anne Midy of CasaMidi, San Miguel Allende

Library and Archives Canada Cataloguing in Publication
Ross, Jane, 1942-, author
Includes bibliographical references.

ISBN: 9781988440804

1. Ross, Jane, 1942- Travel—Middle East.
2. Middle East—Social life, travel and customs.
3. Middle East—Landscape. 4. Middle East - Home
        For information and permission: contact:
        Jane Ross Box 1581, Camrose, Alberta, Canada T4V 1X4
        E: source21@telus.net www.JaneRoss.ca

The ongoing publishing activities of Bayeux Arts Digital – Traditional Publishing
under its varied imprints are supported by the Government of Alberta, Alberta
Multimedia Development Fund, and the Government of Canada through the
Book Publishing Industry Development Program.

Canadian   Patrimoine
Heritage   canadien

For my nephew,
Steven Pattison

FOREWORD

I met Jane Ross in 2003 just after I had just opened XVA Gallery and Art Hotel in Dubai's historical Bastakiya area. She surprised me one day by wanting to interview me for my business acumen in a film she was making about global business. This was a surprise since I felt I knew little on the subject! My business motto then and now is "one day at a time." Yet she was fascinated to know more and our communication continues still. She puts meaning to "keeping in touch." Each invitation for our art exhibitions worthy of a response from Jane is a spark of joy for us at XVA as they are always thoughtfully written in a language rich with meaning and insight — as you will see here in this wonderful book, *Green Parrots in my Garden*.

Allah hum d'Allah, for Jane Ross and her mastery of telling stories, such as of the sidr tree that blessed and expanded her, and for being an oracle of the art of being human.

Green Parrots in my Garden is full of insights into the museums in her mind as she offers us a curated tour through her poems. Jane has expanded my sense of reality offering the possibility of exposing the numina of this place I call home. She inspires me to learn from the bougainvillea, to imagine leaving Dubai and missing heartfelt offers in simple questions like "Madam, may I help you?" She has created a sillage that comes through a window in the wall — along with an open window into the museum in her glowing mind — and is evident of the efficacy in all she does.

Mona Hauser
Dubai
United Arab Emirates

Owner XVA
Gallery, Hotel & Cafe
www.xvahotel.com

The Ocean Refuses No River

**Map: Artist rendering of an antique map
of the Persian Gulf and United Arab Emirates**
by Naz Sharokh

*Maps are not just two-dimensional
pieces of paper depicting geographies,
but documents which, like poetry, contain untold
stories of adventure, promise, memory and hope.*

CONTENTS

Amazing Grace

Our parents often reminded my sister and me that
— Grace is unmerited favour —
God's favour, there and operative in our daily lives
whether we are mindful of it or not.
Life at home — or in foreign lands — has awakened me to
the grace all around me. In all its many forms, grace is amazing.

Land & Sea

Sticks & Stones

Creatures Great & Small

Rose & Thorn

Perfumes & Chypres

Body & Soul

PREFACE

Green Parrots in my Garden emerged from the years I spent with
my husband, Jack Ross, in the Arab and extended Middle East. It also
emerged in part from *my Arabiya, Journey into the New Millennium*
(2021). I felt there was more to follow from the Middle East experiences
and the prose of the first book. The green parrots continued actively in
the museums of my mind until Thanksgiving Day, 2019, when I decided
to write poems set in the Arab Peninsula.

In my life journey I try to understand the beliefs and practices of others.
My *essaie* (French: essayer - to try) sharpened as I journeyed into
Arab lands and the beliefs of the people who live there. Accordingly,
these poems try to capture what that world held and holds for me: the
constellation of people, landscape, religion, weather and cultures. The
experiences of life in the Gulf region stretched and enlarged my sense
of what is possible and/or real; they warmed me with friendship and
nourished me with food. They uplifted me with kindness, grace and
perfume. At times they also troubled me with concepts of fatwa and
threats of war and, most recently, of pandemic. The blessings of that life
amaze me and give rise to the poems in this volume.

*Arab identity revolves in part around the letters of Arabic script. In the
labyrinths of time, experiences were first related in oral language and
later in the lovely symbols of Arabic script where belief, message and art
combine in their own unique alphabet. And so, my poems.*

—Jane Ross, January 30, 2021
Story's Way, Battle River
Alberta, Canada

On Alphabet and Language

Arab calligraphy is both an elegant art and religious form which brings mind, belief and artistic expression together. Like Arab society, the alphabet is relational as characters join to sharpen intent and shape meaning.

It is a beautiful script with balance between its vertical shafts, open curves and arabesques — it is perfect for expressing the language of every day as well as for conveying the messages of ancient manuscripts written in gold leaf on fine vellum. A reed pen with an angled working point enables myriad inflections within the artistic forms of the letters and their harmonious proportions. They capture the beauty, essence and alchemy of ancient history, divine word and nature: each rendering a numinous manifestation of the sacred combined with the human quest *for* the sacred.

> *A printed alembic architecture of light recorded*
> *on palm stalk, on camel's shoulder-bone or*
> *held in memory;*
> *copied to parchment and*
> *swaddled in a green cloth.*

As part of the Arabic language, calligraphy is an expression of the highest art — the art of language and spoken word, combining and continuing the transmission of thoughts and history.

Amazing Grace

Evidence of things unseen

Genesis

As I sat in my garden that morning sipping my coffee,
The green parrots flying in and out of the garden
were more active than usual.
I felt they were trying to tell me something.
Eventually they persuaded me to listen and
to fetch my green notebook
its cover matching their own green colour.
I felt they wanted me to start writing.

As I brushed the sand and dust from the pages,
fragments of my experiences in the desert began to emerge.
By the time the sun reminded me once again
of its inescapable heat, the parrots were gone and
a pattern of words had
formed on the pages of the green book.

Silence

Sounds of silence and Songs of silence
Where does one become the Other?
I do not know. But to find the
wealth in each I must clear
a way for them. Make a place so
inner springs can swell from
pools of light sequestered in spaces where
life surges from substance and spirit matters.
I am human, I cannot live on bread alone.

The Garden is Lovely

American Colony, Jerusalem 1985
The garden is lovely — hydrangeas and geraniums
A tall palm tree stretches to the sky,
Has grown well and high above the wall.
It does not need to stretch more, but
Presses on; Still. high, high and high.
A lesson to be gained from its own
Nature: Stretch to achieve the necessary height. Continue.
Stretch. Above and beyond. Bringing grace and (pro)portion
In the garden of your life.

Many other things are growing here — ideas and words
There is a cyprus tree at the other end of the garden. It too is tall
And bushy. But why only two trees in this garden?
Does the palm attract more attention than the cypress?
Or the philodendron.
A very orange orange hangs bright on a bush,
One amongst many green oranges.
Pots adorn columns. Red flowers respond to the wind.
A coronet crowning the garden
Against the scent of a clear blue sky.

Such a lovely garden. Surprises here — a hotel
In its beginning a home for a sheikh and his harem, became
A stopping place for pilgrims travelling to the Holy Land.
Palestine. Then is not now. Today is conflicted.
Yet. Ancient tree presses on. Stretches higher
when thinkers meet, where thoughts contend, and as writers write.

But in this garden
My father thought. And I thought he would die.
But that was not to be. A few hours later, he was on a tour bus
Comfortable with strangers, enjoying travel in a Holy Land and
I on a plane for London.

Joining the genius of bougainvillea whose minute white flowers are
protected by paper-thin petals of exuberant colour, we can learn.
Find more pleasure as they flaunt their way up, over, and
around the other plants in the garden.
Twining and branching their way in vivid colours,
they tell stories all their very own.

Mother Lullaby

When you were small and just a touch away
I covered you with blankets against the cool night air.

But now that you are tall and out of reach,
I stretch out my hands, cover you with my prayers.

I reach for you with poetry and mystery;
Urge constancy of purpose.

Remind you of your place,
your history, your home and your land.

Remember the Prophet's message:
Paradise is under your mother's feet.

Touches you with songs of nations, religion, and love,
brings spirit worlds together in a single place.

Early Morning Walks

Some mornings lured me deep inside the silence of the date groves
Places reminiscent of ancient times where I walked high on
stone pathways dividing one garden bed from another.

Dirt-topped pathways made of stones wrested from the land
Following ancient *felaj* channels carrying water through
small oases with date groves and gardens.

Sometimes I returned to the groves later in the day for their welcoming cooler
temperatures, at least 10 to 15 degrees less than on the near-by plain or inside
my sun-baked house.

When I longed for flowers in this remote desert place, I turned to the soft
white loveliness of sweet potato blossoms growing under the cooling shade of
palm canopies high overhead.

Sometimes on that stony walkway I would meet a farm woman
brightly dressed and with a huge load of freshly cut grass on her head.
Up with the dawn, she had gathered food for her family of goats.

Sometimes I followed the wadi bed in the direction of Al Mazaheet village
about a mile distant from our compound. Set deep amongst boulders
Sipped rose-flavoured coffee from tiny glass cups with neighbour women.

Glorious on the Garden Wall

There's much to love about bougainvillea against hot desert sand.
Welcome emissaries, they refresh the spirit,
their bright colours help relieve the scorch of heat on hot concrete.

The bougainvillea in our compound grow high and thick,
are awnings of colour and curtains of hot pink, fuchsia, and orange.
Entwined and entwining around the compound wall, they grow
ever thicker until we cannot see who or what lies beyond.

As I struggle with the environment, I learn how to transform
the patch of desert sand inside our compound walls into
a place of refuge, comfort, and even whimsy.
I am charmed, assisted, and encouraged by the bougainvillea.

They respond to my attention—thrust their gorgeous colours in a steady
advance—undaunted in their apparent mission to decorate,
curtain and bring beauty. So, why not learn from them?

Twining and branching their way in vivid colours, we can learn and
find more pleasure as they scramble and flaunt their way up, over, and
around the other plants in the garden.

Dance with the wind. Throw back the dust.
Colour the sand-daubed world!
Capture their energies and engage their excess as a foil for
the layers of heat and desert dust around me.

While the daily news of expanding Iraq war makes life confusing,
the beauty and energy of the flowers helps me adapt to impending change and
find comfort in the conditions around me.
Helps me move past fear with glorious colours of the garden wall.

Jasmine

Each morning my garden was redolent with the scent of jasmine,
an oasis in the hot sand beyond the walls of Villa al Felaj.

In this dry place, plants responded to my care
Rewarded me with their growth and beauty.

Neither profuse nor abundant, but enough.
Together, we did the best that we could do.

Just under the garden wall, the jasmine seemed happy to
grow as well as they could.

Scents from a single white jasmine can change the atmosphere
of a room, shift emotions around a table.

The gift of jasmine moves relationships forward
Activates blessing, binds people together.

The beauty of a jasmine necklace purchased for only a few cents
Revives the spirit of those who are weary.

Listening to the message of the winds,
I am drawn to an alphabet of jasmine and roses,
and to words redolent with nectar and perfume.

Madam May We Help You?

Only a few minutes walk from our compound, the garbage dump was where
I found marble tiles, sandblasted chairs and much more.
Material for repurposing into forms guided by my imagination.

On one such hunting and gathering session the garbage collectors
stopped their truck to ask politely and curiously:
"Madam, may we help you?" I was carrying large marble tiles.

That was the start of it; an unexpected and happy relationship with
unanticipated benefits that made the collection of found things
much easier for me. My new helpers seemed to enjoy it too.

Thereafter, when they found discarded items they thought I might like,
they dropped them off at my place. And I became a furniture designer.
With an ironmonger nearby, the possibilities were endless.

He could make frames for tile tables of various shapes and sizes;
garden ornamentation and even holders for the water hoses that
snake across the garden. Here in Alberta I miss my helpers and scroungers.

I settle with a sun bleached and sand blasted wood chair. When I found it,
it was like a camel's skull, the colour of hot sand. Cleaned up, it has
the colour and patina of pearl. Infused with memories of desert wind
its skin speaks of deep mountain mysteries and of the rocks within its bones.

Three Graces

The gladdest moments in life entwine with departures into the unknown.
Travelling to distant lands is about the shaking off of

Habit (fetters),
Routine (weights as heavy as lead),
Cares (as cloaks familiar).

Journey makes the blood run fast.

Appeals to Imagination,
Awakens Memory,
Engages Hope.

Three graces in the art of human being
Three graces for living life richly.

Journey into Arabiya sharpened my eye and stretched my mind
Offered fragments of experience more than straightforward narrative.

Fragments, like nomadic wanderings,
to experience in new ways and in new orders.
Find words, create meanings. Respond to calling.
Reach back across millennia
to clay tablets and the dawn of civilization.

Grace at the Heart of Journey

Arriving, I am astonished by the beauty of balmy night
the wide, well lit roads edged with masses of flowers, artful road signs, and
the shapes of graceful people gliding by;
Women in flowing long black abeya and
Men in long white *dishdasha*.

The scent of exotic perfumes is thick in the warm night air,
prepares me for life in an ancient desert settlement;
opens my understanding of the region and its people;
provides unending opportunities for reflection and meditation as
I discover graces at the heart of the journey and
along its awe-inspiring ways.

Travel

Why do people travel?
Some to reach a destination, but
in the Arab way, the voyage is an end in itself,
a journey that never ends.
Composed of fragments,
the destination is never reached.

The story—never ends—its narratives live on — and
like the wind and the sand, they
shift and shape, fade and return.

Long Time Away

Madam, you have been a long time away.

I did not recognize the Taliban taxi driver speaking to me.
Yes, for several months; away in Canada with my Mother
who is sick and needed me.
His response was gentle with sympathy and a kind offer
Madam, please let me carry you.

With travel and life abroad comes pleasure,
but also the pains of separation.
What drives these forays into distant lands?
What forces deeply at play, drawing
such different people together in unexpected places,
in encounters that are sweet and life changing?

Encounters that make us better, richer, wiser and kinder.
I have learned from my journeys.
Gained a grander view that sweeps from
simple life beginnings to forms beautiful and wonderfully evolved.
Yes, in the end we arrive at the beginning,
at the places from where we started.

Mr. Amin

It all started with carpets. Persian carpets.
Mr. Amin from Yemen was a carpet salesman,
a colporteur, not of books, but of carpets.
He travelled to nearby Iran to buy carpets and returned to
build clientele around foreigners who did his marketing for him.

Professor Lydia introduced us to Mr. Amin and his carpets.
We were soon to discover his business model as well.
He would call, asking to bring carpets.

"You want carpets? I have nice ones: Tabriz, Isfahan; I can come."

He would arrive with flashing Yemeni eyes and carpets.
A simple and gentle man with a complex carpet business
who liked nothing better than to stay and visit.

Today I reflect on his and other friendships,
how their memory continues to flow like warm water in a felaj.
Are made more powerful in a world made small by technology and travel.
I like to think how friends can help us expand beyond prisons of gray to enjoy
beauty from unexpected sources and in
all the colours of Mr. Amin's Persian carpets.

Zarrah is My Name

"What is your name?"

The exchange of a greeting, what a difference it makes!
While language limitations keep us apart, even small efforts
encourage and warm me in a spiritual way;
yield respect in the presence of war.

We long for things to go well in the world.
Make us think about the milk of human kindness;
its importance. Nourishing.
Minimizing cultural gaps. Dispelling fears.
Causing hope to spring forth.

In days like these Zarrah
makes me more hopeful.
refreshes me with friendship.

This, much better than the war that smells of sweat, and of
burning oil, diesel fuel and spent gunpowder.
Only 800 miles from the action, this morning is hot, the sky is overcast, and
the wind drives sand about.

Metamorphosis

I want to follow the trails of Abraham and Sarah
Beyond water and oasis, to find a shell with a pearl inside,
track through shifting sands leading to a
hidden cave sequestered in a valley of shimmering light.

At first, I did not like the compounds of our desert homes.
I resisted them, felt hemmed in, contained.
But with exposure to the desert and its elements
I learned how compounds offer protection from the wind and
the ever-blowing sand with its cutting grit.

I learned how compounds can be a
harbour of calm in a sandy world; and
how to live with the desert stretching beyond the compound gate.

Like the proverbial ugly duckling, our compound had aspirations
more in line with being a swan. No matter what we did,
the sewer area inside Villa al Felaj compound was a problem.
Humans are created to create and recreate.

I met the Iraqi ceramic handler at Global Village 2002, from him
I bought a plaque to hang outside our front door.
An amazing piece crafted from Euphrates river clay,
It spoke of Sumer and ancient civilizations — and of
grave disruptions in the gardens of Babylon today.

There on the wall entering our house, the plaque did its perfect work.
Silent and colourful, attesting to Biblical times and age-old tensions.
I thought of the Iraqi man, wanted to see him again.
I wanted to tell him about the social impacts of his creation.
When I looked for him again in 2003, he was not there.

Amidst growing regional turmoil and turbulence,
his plaque became ever more valuable to me.
But the story does not stop there.

One day, the plaque was missing from the wall.
Had someone else found it lovely?
Had it been taken by a visitor to our home?
Was its removal based on long-standing animosities?
I cannot judge but I do wonder.

To this day I miss that beautiful work of art and mourn the causes for its loss.
Memory pushes wonderment about deceits at all levels,
about the vying of nations and the ways in which political actions
intercept and redirect human purposes that are right and good,
makes me ponder treachery and reach for new words.

Bedouin Tea

It's a fast track, life in the modern UAE
Where desert people with nostalgia for the past
muse of times when they were at home
with oryx and gazelle; with ibix, falcon and fox;
of their lives close with camel and goat
of hunting at night, when game birds took flight
from their homes in shaded shrub;
when rain meant the greening of desert pastures.
of herbs awakening for gathering, for boiling and drinking.
Oh, the sweet taste and oh the sweet memories of
the desert and Bedouin tea.

N Sha' Allah

Life is not free from pain and sorrow.
If God wills — *N sha' Allah* — since time began
Further than the future; deeper than the past.

God in everything — good or bad.
God wills. *N sha' Allah*. God controls.
Infers resignation to sorrow and pain.

God's blessing or curse, extends to everyone.
Invokes higher power on every thing: sacred or secular.
Connects with the non-material world.

It is not only the spoken word, but also the way
sounds fall from the tongue, remind how life and actions
depend on something greater; ephemeral; eternal.

Laden with meaning; expressed or felt,
a phrase that awakens, binds people and places together,
serves the Covid generation well.

N sha' Allah.
I like to use it myself.

Season of Love and Light

To celebrate the completion of my sixth decade and
the beginning of my seventh
I wished an evening of Beluga caviar, blini and champagne.
A Persian dinner with my love, just the two of us in a setting
with carpets and copper and bronze, with roses and rose waters.

To drink from exquisite glasses etched with gold
To feast on chicken and okra and figs cooked slow and succulent
with oven-fresh flat breads baked near our table
with baba ghanouj perfectly smoky in flavour, and
a cake — just for me.

Though war was imminent, the place was warm and human
and lovely like a desert night.
My choice of place to end one decade and start another
evoked strong emotions, stirred deeply inside me with
palpable connections for dark and perilous times.

A bracelet of crystals, my beloved's gift to me
Precious like light in a dark place,
symbols bringing meanings to life. And yes,
there was the birthday song; sung by Persians and Arabs.
My seventh decade for living well could not have started better.

Land & Sea

Miracles incarnate

Back of the Desert

The road to our house was sandy and rough.
With large boulders remaining from whatever
forces had deposited them aeons ago.
Occasional sand-coloured flat-roofed houses and shops
scattered along the way.
Scraggly black and white goats roamed freely about,
nibbling at whatever they could find.
Sharp black mountains, seemingly impenetrable,
loomed almost directly behind.

And then, for endless terrain beyond . . . the desert.
Can you imagine how beautiful the desert can be?
The light sometimes intense and yellow,
often soft; brushed with haze and mist.
And after the wind, the sand
in fresh configurations
has an allure all its own.

Wadi

When the poor and needy seek water and there is none, and
their tongues are parched with thirst, I, the Lord, will answer them;
I will not forsake them.
I will pour water on them who are thirsty;
I will pour floods upon the dry land,
bring gifts to open hearts.

Dried out waterbeds in mountain valleys
lead out, fill quickly after rain when
water floods through and over them.

Look for depressions in gravel or sandy mounds
piled high with stones and gravel
traversing and intersecting the stony plains of Oman.

But not all wadis are harsh and dry.
Some are always with water
lovely pools of blue, emerald, and azure. Cool.
Lush and verdant with oases of date palms,
grass, and flowering shrubs.

One mystery leads to others
nourished by underground waters
heavy in the company of ancient species
Water poured out on the wadi floor.

A Different Kind of Desert

This desert. A different kind of desert than I had imagined.
I know the Sahara; have traveled on its bosom.
But this, this is a different desert.
A hotter, drier, more foreign desert with
stark rocky outcroppings and remote villages.
A vast desert offering secluded pockets where one is alone with the heat, and
vulnerable to its powerful presence.
More ancient, prescient with jinns in a liminal space between
the temporal human and spirit worlds,
reminiscent of the Old Testament and its murky rituals.

A scorched and stony place. Dry. Altogether dry except when rains gather;
announce their unexpected arrival with a clap of thunder
inform about the deluge on its way.

A short distance beyond our compound,
black mountains erupt from a flat acacia-dotted stony plain.
Yet only a half-hour inland from where the desert gives way to
warm Gulf waters that dip ever so gently away from the land.
You can wade in these waters—out and out and out;
watch fish as they swim around your feet.

I feel it. I hear it. The sounds of wind grating and churning . . .
sometimes playing at my feet, sometimes crunching, but
always moaning through the mountain tunnels nearby.

In this strange desert plain at the foot of the black mountains,
I thought about my ancestors and their journey to an unknown land.
Their land was rough and forested. Cold.
Mine is rough and confounding. Hot.
They stayed and created a new life. I left and tend now to remember;
listen to the wind; pay attention to the museums in my mind;
select words to retrace and recreate those experiences.

Entering into that transformative life was at once exotic and difficult.
Unexpected the new sounds; sometimes with great silence,
sometimes wind tearing on rock, or the incessant irritations of
rocks grating and grinding.

A place where the sand is coarse and granular.
Small bits, large bits find their way into everything.
The fridge door opens with squeak and grind. Sand on metal . . .
The car door opens with squeak and grind. More sand on metal.
Dry grindings of hard surfaces against hard surfaces. Even walking is difficult;
there is sand in my shoes, with stones that cut. My ankles twist and groan.
As the Old Testament instructs,
I must take care lest I dash my foot on a stone.

Mysteries in Sand

Reading William Blake I return to the desert
Try to understand its profound mysteries,
Try to find the world in a single grain of sand, then
Watch how it gathers, leaps on the wind. Incandescent.
Learn how, like snowflakes, each grain has a story to tell.
Marvel how it builds — dunes extending for hundreds of miles.

Sometimes concave, sometimes convex,
always spectacular, ever changing, ever reshaped by the wind.
Sometimes with dense storms erasing all visibility, or
with drifts fastening man and beast in its thrall.

This is no monochrome desert;
you will find no drab here, but stories
written in molten sand with vibrant colours.
Biblical legends with angels in purple and scarlet.

The mysteries of sand do not escape the artist's reach, yield kaleidoscopes that
flow in bottles or between layers of glass, or present as icons in windows;
Tell the good news. God is with us.

Marc Chagall brings allegories in glass. In his windows, the beauty of sand
shines through, captures light, displays mysteries in stains of exceptional colour.
Demonstrates how well things can go when creation is from the heart.

Transformed from sand, this glass reminds how land merges with spirit
Is dramatic, multi-hued and of stunning intensities; speaks to the soul in
flaming orange, deep purple, emerald and cobalt.

In Arabiya, each Emirate has its own colour of sand:
>Fujairah sand is red. Dramatic.
>Sharjah sand is fallow. Tawny dark.
>Dubai sand is beige. Light.
>Ras al Khaimah sand is yellow. Like gold and papyrus.
>Abu Dhabi sand is white. The colour of worship.
>Ajman sands tend towards old silver, while
>Sand in Garden City Al Ain is green. Fertile.

I love the spectacular configurations of sand in Nature where,
in response to the light of sun by day and that of the moon at night,
the sand takes on colours that defy description.
Much for the mind *and* the mind's eye, but surfeit for the hand and its
bold attempts to paint in words or in oil, or with pigment and water.

Out on the desert where wind shifts sand without cease,
there is beauty of other kinds.
Awake at dawn to find the desert brushed clean except
for the tracks of the desert's night creatures. While one millennium
merges into the next, desert creatures are alive and active . . .
>barb-tail lizards, yellow snakes, scorpions, camel spiders, mice and rats
>creatures with wings that collect moisture in their anatomical cups
>all part of creation not known to those who frequent only the day.

Tell me. Does nature know any boundaries in its adaptive creations?
From soft to fabulous and stark, yields glimpses through mists of custom;
transforms us in its wisdom to worship and delight.

Musandam

Norway of the East

How to describe the stunning scenery and mood of
this remote Omani tip of the Arabian Peninsula?
On the Strait of Hormuz, this wilderness land seems at odds with the
stretch of open water between peninsula and Iran.

With frequent saber rattling and threats of closing the Strait,
Iran seems to enjoy its capricious hold on world oil supply and economy, and
finding ways to move simple goods to remote communities along
the coast of nearby countries Oman and UAE.

There is much about Musandam that made us want to go there. Often.
There were no fine hotels or restaurants then.
No Zighy Bay Resort; designed for the six senses, but with
more than enough culture and place to stimulate our senses combined.
A picnic lunch and a good supply of water carried us through the day.

The curvaceous coastal highway north from Sharjah and Ajman offers
a journey in touch with the sea on one side and with
steep mountains on the other. Roads off the main highway offer
spine-tingling curves, wind up, down, around and over the mountains;
turn sharply; go east to go west, and south to go north.
There are no guardrails here.

Occasionally there is evidence of human habitation.
Around one corner on a high rocky road, an ancient settlement tucked under a
huge outcropping of mountain. Protective.
When we stop, kohl-rimmed female eyes peer back suspiciously
through narrow slits in the beaked black *niqab*.
Are these looks defiant and hostile, or simply curious?
How long will the lifestyle of these women prevail?
Dubai is not far away and television is already in their homes.

Earlier in the day, lambs, goats, and clay pots arrived from Iran
on small boats operating along the coasts of Oman and Emirates.
I bought a large white clay pot for one dollar. Splendid.
I did not think to ask the price of a goat or a lamb.

Market over, off into the night the little boats sped,
grouped together for their short night journey to a secluded Iranian port.
This is risky, dark business but profitable — like black markets anywhere.
Seemingly at odds with private bays, majestic mountains and fjords. Quiet.

In just a few short years, this mix is of majesty and grandeur,
wilderness and glitz, of privacy and luxury,
a resort with personal butlers and designer body care
all — for only $8,000 a day.

Jewels of the Desert Night

I am drawn to the jewels of the desert night,
its warm velvet sky, its vast silence,
the scent of wild oregano on hot sand and how customs
shape relationships that separate or bind people together.

Magical variations on night laid down over eons of time.
Rhythms in the black sky — numinous and lively
A language all its own; this grammar and precious experience.

The feel of true night. Long, dark travel high over the desert is as
dark as night should be on a moonless night.
Inky dark. Dark like squid. Night dark.

Women's fashion inspired by the dark beauty of desert night,
by the sweet terror of kohl, by the glitter of light spread like
a necklace on the black desert – or by the warm light of desert moon.

The garments flow, as does the *sillage*, that trail of perfumes
wearers leave behind them as they move,
the scent of women flows; supple, confident and graceful
imprinted with the flash of desert culture and fierce with desert pride.

Rain

Rain is rare in these parts. Returning from Musandam, it poured.
At times we felt we were sliding down the mountain rather than driving.

When strong waters gushed over the road,
We thought we would spend the night in that remote dark place.

But storms are quick and fierce here.
On our way once more, another surprise awaiting.

There in the great space of seeming nowhere, a military barricade with
Kindly guards who said there was no way through.

We would have to return — back from where we had come.
They knew and so did we, the impossibility of that journey.

And so, with conversation the only exchange,
Broke rules, gave us safe crossing and blessing.

Baraka.

Seafaring

Coastal waters plied for centuries.
Journeys of long ago,
as long as a thousand years and more,
when Gulf sailors reached as far as China.

Journeys possible by navigational devices that
could chart the Pole Star above the horizon.

A time when Arabs, sensitive to
the forces of the heavens,
the earth and the seas, were
lured beyond shores familiar
to search and to find.

What quest this?
Fragments tell part of their stories;
of unfathomable stretches that can
be reached only by imagination.

Window in the Sea

There is a window in the open sea
Where silver birds search for treasure and
Turquoise islands wait.

Mariners
Cannot resist this ancient pull of place
Travel by dhow
Crafted of teak from Zanzibar.

Mariners
Cannot resist lure of fragrant distance.
Their boats follow falcons and dolphins.
Their maps connected to clouds and blue stars.

There is a window open in the sea
Where stories from the wind beckon with promise of
Emeralds and pearls that are waiting.

Gulf Tour

By day we drifted on the warm Gulf waters. And
at night were anchored in small coves, lulled to sleep by
the sound of water lapping on our boat.

Ringed in by sharp brown mountains that
towered around and above us, it was a time and place where
we felt alone in the world.

We mused aloud to each other, tried to comprehend the wonder.
We swam in a little bay, played in the waters and took time to walk on the
rim of shore before sharp mountains leaping up ever straight and ever up.

These are no mountains for climbing! Only rock and vertical cliffs where falcons
live, breed, nest and bear their young. Do they understand the ancient codes
etched in their genes and connected to their rocky home?

A trip complete with Indian chefs with divine creations
Fresh fish and tuna, sprinkled with lime juice and grilled. Rice with sumac
and saffron. Salads, fruits, and sweet meats; and always with coffee.

Jumeirah

An oasis. Inside its cool embrace, wave-patterned carpets
resonate like Jacob's coat of many colours,
spread richly through corridors,
offer promise for that which lies within the waiting rooms.

Gulf waters swirl at the feet of
dish-dashed men
      immaculate in flowing white gowns scented with blossoms
      dealing in the prices of oil
local women
      gorgeous in black with lace the colour of desert night
      shopping without their men;
      Slavic models
      confident in pricey shoes designed for seduction
      luring with their eyes, preying with their bodies.

Amidst these people who mingle with ease,
my head swirls, tries to patch contradictions, bind together
      the counterpoint of harsh and elegant;
      of shy and vibrant colours;
      of harsh demands and desert calm.

But Jumeirah oasis is only a resting spot,
the desert beckons, offers promise of other worlds to know.

Red Stars for Supper

Each of us inherits a treasure house of wonders, and
when we engage creatively in life
we enable a signature; a taste and
an imprint of our own and others to emerge.

In the mystery of individual experience
a rich harvest of possibilities awaits.
Arab cultures invite modern pilgrims inside
the treasures within our bones and
the wonder of shining red stars for supper.

Sticks & Stones

Cradles of history

Cradle of History

Sometimes we passed small dwellings tucked into this cradle of history.
Perched on small rock ledges of mountains rising abruptly behind them,
some are ruins from earlier times — some are resting places for visiting.

Weather is cooler here, but life is harder.
In these narrow passages
daylight comes late and sunset comes early.
A sublime landscape with danger when
rain in the high mountains brings vengeance,
wipes out trees, and piles more rocks in their wake.

We stopped for coffee and dates at a village twenty-eight kilometres in.
This meant parking the car on a widening of the already narrow road
cut out as a cleft in the mountain that rose steep and upwards on one side.
On the other side, an area carved out for human habitation,
a place where history gives way to rugged myths from long ago.

Theirs is a remote social world, obliged to receive strangers,
to offer them coffee and dates.
Our visit went well until a small whiff of cloud appeared in the hot sky.
Congeniality collapsed as tension leapt in our midst.
Our driver warned of the need to get out, be ready to find high ground;
escape the rain that comes so very fast and dangerous.

Desert Architecture

Ancient structures of coral-impregnated plaster,
shield from sun, from wind and blowing sand
Made from materials at hand, they are lovely to the eye
Wrought from the desert and the sea, have a language all their own.

Stone, wood and coral *can* and *do* speak of
desert construction responding to weather;
find ways to accommodate its vagaries;
reveal the mind of desert dwellers, offer shelter and habitation.

The concrete of modern construction does not respond to climate.
Absorbs heat all day; drills heat inwards with confounding intensity
ejects its miserable accumulation into concrete spaces.

I prefer structures
with cooling wind tunnels that
move hot air upwards and
through felaj channels of soothing water
flowing within and around.

Habitations once fallen into ruin are fashionable again.
Lure the eye and spirit — back to different ways of building and living.
Decorative and functional, bearing the lovely names of *areesh* and *barasti*,
they are remarkable; speak of nature as provider and wise teacher.

The Roads of Oman

Each Oman road marker is an inscription at a particular place,
not an intrusion on the deserts or in the mountains.
The Sultan imagined ways of making road system and signage elegant,
epic, exploratory, and even sensuous; some roads
a long caress through desert spaces.
Instructions inform; teach history and geography; tell stories:

Turn right at *Book Roundabout*
        (between Muscat and the road to Rustaq);

When you come to *Treasure Chest Roundabout*
        (remember Ali Baba's Box) turn left;

At *Fort Roundabout* head up-country and into the desert
        (remember history of protectionism);

Water Pot Roundabout reminds that
        water is valued in a land where water is scarce;

Clock Roundabout shows how
        modernization has encroached on eons of time;

Dhow Roundabout tells a proud seafaring history
        with Zanzibar and other places;

Oryx Roundabout emphasizes the need to
        protect the oryx and other desert animals.

At *Incense Burner Roundabout* head into Muscat;
        perfume is never far away,
        suggests the importance of scent and
        the rituals of hospitality.

The road to Al Bustan Palace reminds of transportation histories.
Stone-age bodies, desert bodies, discovering speed; discovering distance,
space and the magic of a traffic circle to direct and connect.
Highway markers go beyond signage, become works of art.

        Road signs as icons of culture, creativity, and places.
        What a welcome practice. Discovery and delight.
        There are lessons here for highway makers of the world.
        Why not offer celebration along roadways
        Enable travelers to see and to learn and to understand
        the places through which they pass?

Nizwa

We approached Nizwa as dawn was breaking.
From high afar, we had seen the lights, but it was a long way down.
Down, down and down. Switchbacks: forth and back and back and forth. Down,
down, down. A journey like no other!

Time present — Time past: An ancient city;
a long, modern city with an oasis stretching for miles along
wadis with water from the high mountains.
More than twelve years in the building of it all:
great round towers, forts, gardens, museums, and markets,
especially the antique and cattle markets.

We are tired from our night on the mountains,
so first a shower and a nap.
Jack is keen to show me where he found
the hand forged copper pot he gave me when
I joined him at the dawn of the new millennium.

The Hajar Mountains are still in my bones;
that remarkable mix of old forms
adapted for new functions.
I remember high mountains where
fire meets the rose and life gives way to
new variations on desert life and its meanings.

Blue Souq

Souq of souqs. Blue Souq of Sharjah with
millions of tiles glistening in all the colours of blue.
A magnificent complex where desert wind towers create
unforgettable images on the desert sands.

Water blue. Sky blue. Day blue. Night blues that deepen into
charcoal blue and the dark hues of indigo and lapis lazuli.

In the mythology of blue, its power seeps through
everything that is Arab and Persian.

Romance the stone. Discover Rubaiyat in merchant stories
Find kingdoms in Persian miniatures.

Depart to the far horizons.
Learn to trust things that glitter.

⌒

Treasure-seeking travelers stop.
With Sharjah Blue Souk nearby,
who needs other sources of entertainment?

Burj al Arab

Arrive with anticipation. Leave in awe.
Be inspired. Love a place that is stylish. Enormous. Iconic.
Embrace a new monument that evokes wonder, inspires meditation.

Create a daring new place — a tower of two worlds.
Let orient and occident come together. Dance a new song of
Ancient and modern, of sea and land, of delicate and bold.
See them come together, explode with fittings of crystal and gold.

Arrive in the sunlight, or just before dusk
Either way, there's room to luxuriate in the magnificent:
Gulf laid out forever on one side; and
Desert on the other, equally laid out forever.

Let there be rooms that travel down without changing direction.
Fill with surprises and endless delight. When daylight vanishes
Embrace an Arab night; the magic of a dark sky and
The warmth of conversation in good company.

Feast on olives the size of kiwi, stuffed with haloumi and nuts.
Feast on fresh bread and *baba ghanouj*,
its smoky taste nearing perfection.
Sip apricot nectar and bathe the scent of a thousand perfumes.

Let there be sensations and illusions in the colours of the sea:
Active in aqua, turquoise, azure, emerald and more;
Festoon it at night, drape it with swaths of colour
Let there be interplay of textures to locate me at sea.

Let there be stories of a sailboat or a pearling dhow,
Evoke mystery when light dances like veils. See beyond.
Envision a time when shrouds are lifted, give way so
Spirits luminous can be seen, bring body and soul together.

Let it contribute to the making of new legends. How many thousands of
Nights would a modern Shahrazad need to tell the stories?
Forge covenants of imagination and understanding,
Apply knowledge and capture experience.

Let it, like language and stories, reveal place and meanings,
Foster insights with larger patterns; inform present and future with
Fragments that layer and flow together, re/form history and
Fuel covenants for futures of lasting peace.

So then, let us gather together, fathom structure and place.
Dare to dream new dreams.
Fashion icons with a few sweeps of a pen;
Create monuments that nourish and flourish.

Seven Sisters

Before the dawn of this new millennium,
I had not heard their names — the seven Emirati sisters

Abu Dhabi |Ajman | Al Fujairah | Sharjah | Dubai
Umm al Quwain | Ra's al Khaimah

Where there is sun, sun, and more sun.
Clean water and clean beaches. Fabulous hotels.
Epicurean food. The latest fashion.
Sports and culture within easy access.
Shopping, shopping and more shopping.
Glittering malls offer goods from around the world.

Remnants of the past add to the experience.
High in remote villages, tribal women peer through eyes rimmed with *kohl*
behind *borqua*, the mask-like face piece still in use by some women who
live in isolation from the outside behind huge boulders of their mountain homes.

In an instant of time, nomadic Bedu have transferred from
riding camels to driving muscle trucks and designer vehicles.
One feels the testosterone on finely engineered highways connecting
the seven sister towns, villages and cities, and even the remote mountain places.
Where else in the world will you find luxury cars of so many leading designs
— Jaguar, Lamborghini, Rolls Royce, Ferrari —
parked outside your favourite shopping centres on an ordinary shopping night?
Emiratis propelled from camels to luxury cars in less than a generation.

Camel Caravan

Parade of Nations.
Dozens of art camels parade through the city
come alive in brilliant colours and imaginative designs.

This is no ordinary exhibition but an extravaganza in fiberglass,
camels by artists from around the globe, public art that dazzles.

One Canada camel is splendid with mountains, forests and plains; another is
wrapped in a vivid painted version of the Canadian flag.

Gorgeous camels and, like real camels, they are proud.
Life size, each one tells its own story.

They are a multidimensional socio-cultural and geography lesson in
exuberant colours, their designs reflective of countries they represent.

When imaginations kindle in Dubai, the impacts are global and invitational:
Join the parade, experience the glitter and dream new dreams.

Old Bastakiya

Old Bastakiya brings
feelings of other times and other places.
It stirs the imagination and heightens the senses,
makes me more attentive to detail and choices to
understand how human habitation in its many forms
stands as a gift to human kind for this new millennium.
In a region characterized by tension,
it is a place where peace is breaking out.

Textile markets, narrow stalls, and moneychangers
remind of earlier times. Bustle with modern rhythms as
people mill about, shift goods from small boats into bazaars along
its narrow streets and inner courts. Restaurants, art galleries, and
museums add richness and colour.

Rescued from ruin, Old Bastakiya is a testament to people of vision
who recognized its value and refused its demise; refused its replacement
by the city exploding just beyond its protective walls.
A colourful, exciting, and transformational place that
opens its ancient doors to new ways of thinking, being and doing.
Wandering its narrow alleys, I sense connections with ancient wind
tunnels and dynamic things . . . happening at the centre.

Jebel Ali

Booming port city atop a hill gently leading to the sea.
Once a garden, named by the Prophet's cousin
No ordinary port this —
      enormous tax-free zone
      home to thousands of global companies.

        "Welcome to UAE Free Zones. Hello.
        Would you like to talk about formation of
        a new company in UAE Free Zones?"

Enter the world of ReExport for thriving port trade
transfer stations for goods moving around the world
their volume and variety unsurpassed.

Stop at Jebel Ali and you see it. Huge container ships glide in and out,
Planes fly in, their cargo offloaded to waiting ships, then on their way again.
Elements working together, a gigantic supply chain of goods and services.
Everything and everybody is on the move.

        Add luxury hotels, great beaches and
        the world's largest desalination plant
        and what do you get? A centre
        prophets could not imagine nor supplicate.

Creatures Great & Small

Beauty in the wilderness

Avifauna

The avifauna of Oman has 494 species
and that of United Arab Emirates has 468
I do not know so many birds; cannot name them
But I am open to learning their ways
Meet them in my garden.

These parrots — green in my garden
Each morning they are there,
appear as in a vision. Then where?
Are they gone — from the far reaches of time?
Returning. Swooping. Chirping and Flitting.

If she appeared as though in a vision, then
from where the long reach of time?
Do they know that
Matter(s) cannot be destroyed. Do not decay,
Re/appear in different forms.

These parrots. Green in my garden
Are new to me. I am more familiar with Black. Crows.
I do not exchange parrots for crows, but
Find ways to expand and adjust the
Sliding together of Desert and Prairie.

Beauty from a High Wilderness

Pashmina, like perfumes, has poetry in its strands,
synonymous with fashion and high-end furnishings.
Valuable. Costly. Pashmina scarves in every colour of the rainbow.

Pashmina in all the colours are beautiful, but it is the natural Pashmina for
which I yearn. Rare and beautiful — the colour of Pashmina.

Speak with reverence. Ever so gently, a real Pashmina scarf is
removed from its place—demonstrates its elusive character;
Filmy and fine it slips through my wedding ring with ease.

What is this beauty and how does it emerge in such harsh conditions?
Can the small mountain goats who yield its delicate fibres tell us?
I want to know. Herdsmen from high Himalayan lands, can you tell us?

Tell us stories of how pashma move together, survive together,
bear burdens together; how the best fibres are found on goats exposed to
the coldest cold; how adaptation yields this magic, this incredible soft.

As for my own Pashmina, one is black and the other the colour of
soft pearl brushed with the light of early morning sun on Gulf waters;
Hushed by the sky of high mountain homes.

A String of Camels

There's a lot to learn about camels.
As for me, I thought my life was in order until
a string of camels
entered and changed everything.

There's a lot to learn about camels.
In the early morning before the heat was up,
I liked to walk on the stony plains under the tall black mountains
behind our compound where it is peaceful but full of
fascinations to observe and experience.

On a perfect morning, my reveries were cut short by camels
several of them heading across the rocky plain in my direction.
Without ideas on how to share a large desert plain with camels,
my flight hormones tore loose, carried me home at
a speed altogether more than I am usually able.
I am not a sprinter. I am hardly even a runner.

There's a lot to learn about camels.
There is prose and mythology and facts.
A gift from Allah, treasured and reverenced
Brutish and nasty — friendly and warm.
Provider and transport for desert people.

Adapted for desert endurance
Camels can go for weeks without food or water.
Double lids protect eyes from blowing sand.
Their eyelashes wipe sand from their eyes and their
nostrils shrink to slips, just big enough for the passage of oxygen.

There's a lot to learn about camels.
Camel milk and camel meat for food.
Camel dung with herbs as poultice for wound dressing.
Camel dung dried for fuel.
Camel hair woven into cloth for garments.

There's a lot to learn about camels.
Steed and burden bearer, resource for human and other species
Its milk sustains life; you can thrive on it with dates and water;
yields beauty potions and alchemies for the sensual lives of desert people.
Step back in time — think about the milk in which Queen Sheba bathed.

Arabiya, what in the world have you wrought in me?
You have made me feel at one with the drift of time . . .
a sip of camel's milk, a river of sensations,
the taste and smell of place, the sprouting of ideas.

Desert Mythology

Some mornings I headed directly out into the stony plain
to watch scarabs that are as black as the mountains behind them. Fascinating
creatures, they are Black Commanders who live in close relationship with
camels and camel droppings.

Commanders to commandeer: the creation of mythology,
the continuation of their lineage; and also to commandeer my curiosity.
Observing scarabs in their labour, I want to know more about them.
What the meaning of these dung beetles?

By the time I came out in the morning, the dung beetles were already
hard at it, busy about their work in the warming heat of the sun;
pushing balls of camel dung along the desert floor
or up small pyramids of sand.

These balls are precious cargo, for inside the dung ball is
where the scarab has laid its eggs.
The action of rolling, compressing the ball until it is
strong enough to bury in the sand, until the baby scarabs hatch.

Egyptian lore explains it was by watching the scarab's practice of
laying their eggs in animal dung and decaying flesh that
early people came to associate the scarab with
rebirth, renewal, and resurrection.

They likened the movement of the sun in its orbit across the sky with the labours of scarab rolling their precious dung balls along.
They mythologized scarabs as representing Kepri, the gigantic scarab who is responsible for the Sun and its actions.

Kepri, who rolls up the Sun from the eastern horizon each morning and supports it in its journey across the sky and guides it to its place of rest on the other end of the world at day's end.
Occupying such an auspicious place, it is recreated and worn.

The creation of new forms and thoughts is
not accomplished by intellect alone, but
by instinct acting from the inner self and necessity.
The creative mind plays with the objects it loves.

Thinking in symbols that are older than human history and
inborn from earliest times, generates intergenerational
nourishment for the human psyche and living life in
harmony with symbols and their inherent wisdom.

Turtle Garden

Turtles bring complex questions about time and creation.
From their ancient worlds confound, fascinate and attract us,
Remind that somewhere a remarkable bonding with
Power shocks us into silence.

Turtles bring complex questions about time and creation.
Make us wonder if the seas are still the
friendly home offering comfort
since the dawn of creation.

For eons, the waters have been a clean home
with the pulse, rhythm, and sounds of water and deep and
with historical depth that defies comprehension of
creatures evolved in the vast unfolding of time.

Contrast the primordial sounds of their ancient water home
with the heavy drone of gigantic ships and their horns,
with the frothing swipe of offshore rigs.

Water and land. Land and water, an alternating cycle that
guides sea turtle life in the sea to lay their eggs on land
Forth onto the land and back into the sea in a
cosmic rhythm that stirs states of meditation and awe.

Nesting on the sand she has a lot of digging to do.
Her task focused and intense, breaks only for rest.
Attuned to creation's call, obedient to another moon
Nothing distracts her, the call is strong.

Her eggs are opalescent orbs. Beautiful.
Like large pearls, they drop, membranous and singular,
one after the other. Her passionate digging. Spell. Binding.
Connecting procreative moments with deep time.

There are tears. Is she crying for the deep memory of Time?
Her work done, she slips back into the sea and
its timeless memory.
Mindful of creation and attuned to its call.

When her infants are born, there is no mother or father around
to tell them what to do. Their own genetic coding carries them off to sea
as fast as their fledgling flipper legs can carry them.
Reaching the water, the sea is their mother.

Goat Friends

Out and about I liked meeting the itinerant goats of the larger
Rustaq area. Since there was seldom anyone to talk with,
the goats made me happy.

They made me wonder about things: like how old is their lineage?
Does this goat family link back to the goats of Biblical times?
Is reflection a regular part of their day?

What about the ancient rituals and stories of sacrifice and redemption?
These experiences required deep listening and
depended on my care to translate the experience into words.

I was especially connected with three female goats who travelled together.
They were proud and confident and haughty, but
graceful and gracious; lovely in their own way.

They seemed to wonder about me too. Curious and persistent,
they ventured in my direction.
Eventually they seemed glad to see me. . .
Just stopping by for tea.

Each morning they made their rounds of the compounds, digging their way through the mounds of plastic garbage bags for possible bits of food or cardboard or anything else they found to be edible.

When I began throwing food scraps to them over our compound wall, their relationship with me warmed considerably.
They were quick to catch on. The scraps did not last long.

The next day my goat friends would be back for more. Our daily visits went on like that for several weeks—until the ceremonial Islamic Eid rituals involving the slaughter of animals—and then

There were no more goat visits. After the celebrations my walks seemed empty without them; their absence suggesting their life's purpose had been served in the rituals of sacrifice and celebration.

Bird Watching

Eros and compassion do not belong
to us as human beings.
Alone.

This morning I saw a baby bird
fall from a tree. The other birds were frantic.
Who, I wonder, cares for humans in their distress?

This morning there is news of people
Falling. In great numbers.
Libya, Egypt, Tunisia, Bahrain. Syria.
Eros and compassion are shared.
Are we ready to care for one another?

Now the news of global pandemic is incessant.
Daily recitations intone what should be done
Cries for help are incessant; instructions are not unified.
How can humans care for one another?
Remind that people matter
Insist that citizens are much
more than tax payers and economies.

Lesson in Love and Birds

The Pakistani ambassador took us to his office window
to watch love birds snuggling and preening.
He explained they are actually small parrots with
the intelligence of larger parrots.

He told stories of their lovemaking and their babies,
of their family life and sweet graces;
how they enrich and warm his life in a foreign land.

When our visit was over,
Maggie was granted her visa to Pakistan and
I left with a treasure trove of sweet memories.

When I hear reports about caldrons of political trouble
bubbling in Pakistan, I return to the ambassador's office and
an experience far more human than bureaucratic.

So let us learn from these birds,
Who know how to love and
how to share their sweet grace.

Oyster Garden and Pearls

The Kingdom of Heaven is called a pearl of great price;
is like unto a merchant who seeks fine pearls, who,
when he found one, sold all he had to buy it.

How do pearls *form* and what do pearls mean?
What does pearling demand?

Great strength for long journeys out to sea
Complex astronomical understanding and navigational skill
Seasonal hunting and gathering; engaging relationships
extended families organized and shifting between coast (subsistence),
desert (horticulture), camel (herding), date (farming) and fishing.
Demands cooperation for boats, labour and profits.

Hunters and gatherers in the sea,
A pearl of great price could sell for fifteen thousand pounds.
Today — a cool half million for a single pearl.
Others, cast aside, are food for oysters.

Seas adorned with white-sailed pearling boats,
a maritime beauty of boats and atmosphere.
Demands a throbbing magic, patterned with songs to
guide the pearlers and lighten their hazardous work.

Beauty in Place

Pearls upon the ocean. What are they?
Perhaps the meaning differs for each of us and
it is the keepers of their memories who know.

Are they drops of rain trapped by oysters at night?
Feathers brushed into the sea by clouds?
A simplification, a gentle joy?

Treasures hid away? Ache of the sea,
a love gift from the gods to humans?
Like perfume, make my mind glow.

Rose & Thorn

Music from solitude

Alone in My Desert Home

This strange house set in a sandy place with boulders all around.
This strange place of compound walls and heat.

I feel alone. Really alone, wonder how I will make a life here.
This strange house is not pretty; the rooms strange
Reflect configurations of sand and mountain.
Everything grates or protests. Is there sand inside of every thing?

There are windows but I cannot see beyond the compound wall.
Black mountains loom high above; dominate everything below.
Puny plants struggle in their sandy hot bed.
Hot wind bites my winter face and whips my hair.
The air is drier than I have ever felt. Sucking dry.
I need moisturizer—lots of it—and a scarf for my head!

⟣

I struggle for words. Need places to put them.
Places where thought can form and land.
Echo meanings from another side. It seems creation is calling.
Bids me understand the meaning of this Empty, alone.
Find words to make meaning,
chronicle life in this strange and foreign land.

While conditions within our compound walls seem safe,
There is increasing fragility of peace across the region.
People are getting anxious. I wonder about the parrots.
Do changing times with threats of war affect them?

Each encounter with the parrots makes me think.
Alone inside the compound walls with them,
it seems they understand my loneliness for my parents,
my sister and my home. I wonder how their families work and
how they sustain family relationships in seasons of change.

Letter to Family

This situation makes me strain to the far reaches of my mind
to find ways of thinking and writing about my experiences here.
They are unusual and dramatic. Even meditative. What their meaning?

Some speak of the desert as barren and empty; as desolation and waste.
     To me it is full.
There is an area called the Empty Quarter.
     To me it is full.
Requires new physics and poetry to describe places and sounds
     beyond description.

     William Carlos Williams understood the desert as
     the music of survival, subdued and half heard.

Sometimes the desert is pathless. Seducing and seductive.
The desert invites penetration. Exploration.
It can be rough and treacherous.
Hot and sucking dry.
With red winds and scorched white land where
sand grits the mouth and makes hair heavy.

At times, cold and miserable. Constantly on the move,
it does not rest except at dawn when there is peace.
After the wind, the desert is silent. Still.
At dawn, its sounds are sounds of silence.
Songs of silence.

Beryl Markham writes how the desert can deceive,
twist perception, alter one's grasp on sanity with
sultry mists and mirages of water and trees.

But, what is "desert" and *which* deserts?

Inhospitable deserts — and uninhabitable broad reaches of
high dunes with deadly quicksand in its valleys.
Home to gazelle, oryx, sand cats and spiny-tailed lizards
adapted to the desert's harsh conditions.

William Dalrymple explains the desert as
a place where camels lurch along in chains,
move in strangely beautiful, seasick motions as
they break onto the sand dunes.

Home to the Bedou who have lived here for generations,
a place like no other, vast and mesmerizing
where sand dunes shift and heave and seem to roll on forever.

This is an altogether magical place where
sand varies in colour from orange to rich reds and
stunning mixtures of purple, green, and indigo.
Mixed with tones of ochre and amber, its colours are
like Sidr honey and finest desert gold.

Witness

It's not only the desert that can be extreme.
Storms in this part of the world are often extreme.
Coastal signs warn against swimming during high winds.
But each winter the press reports about people who
drown after heading into rough Gulf waters.

Travelling by taxi on a morning after an extraordinary storm,
the driver and I see an extraordinary thing . . .
a ship thrown far onto the beach.
High tide and night winds
strong enough to hurl the ship onto the land.

What a strange sight this, and what a strange feeling to
drive between the water and the beached ship.
What happened?
What reordering of normal?
A small tsunami perhaps?

Stephen Hawking helps us make sense of vicissitudes
in a universe that is extraordinarily complex.
Hurtling along on my green parrots and garden journey,
I wonder how to patch extremes together;
how to make sense of the senseless.

I think of Chinua Achebe and
how he frames complexity in his writing:
Tackles the unseemliness.
Things fall apart.
Centres cannot hold.

Stephen Hawking helps us put them together again.
Claims integration of things within a systematic whole.

In the grand scheme of things, things disparate
death, loneliness, blood, rituals, storms, and
the actions of wild animals come together,
are bound together with threads of
inextricable beauty and meaning.

Dry

There are no trees
in this compound.
Only the wind.
Only the desert sand.
Only the scorching sun.
Only the rocks.
Only lunar black mountains.
A frightening composition.

Outings

I enjoy outings with my neighbours at Old Rustaq,
following the felaj into the date plantations and
among the luxuriant date palms.
In the scorching heat, it is cooler there.
Amongst the palms, it is even more comfortable,
with each tree an umbrella to shade from the sun.
Sometimes I simply follow the felaj inside the oases or
sit on their rocky edges, dangling my feet in the cool water while
I watch small black minnows swimming about my feet.

My first outing on the stony plains taught me
the *real* purpose and function of the veil;
not for style or custom, but for protection.
We started in early morning before the sun's searing heat.
By mid-morning, the sun was brutal and the wind furious,
whipping sand into my hair and cutting my face.
Sun, wind, and sand — a frightening combination
Once was enough!
There were no more outings *sans* veil to protect.

Terror in the Garden

—2003—
That day,
it seemed all the world's airplanes were passing overhead.
Low. We felt alarm. Growing.
What? Why the reason for so many?

Gardener Rhahid was more alarmed than we.
He knew the meaning of airplanes overhead
His experience of war was deep.

He grabbed my arm, implored comfort in his distress:
"Oh, Madam, I know the meaning. First you hear them.
Then you see them; the people.
The women. The children — no arms, no legs."

Turning on the television, we caught a single announcement:
hundreds of airplanes scheduled to land in Turkey,
diverted to Dubai airport only a short distance from our compound.

We do not know how or why we caught that single newscast.
There was no further mention of diverted flights,
But the airplanes continued to arrive.

What to do?
In those tense pre-war days
no one knew what to do.
Some were ordered to stay where they were,
either outside the country or inside.
Grounded.

International news was not good.
Some days after the war's onset,
we felt compelled to venture out.

Conditions at the airport were astounding.
The tarmac was full . . .
a gigantic airplane yard with all the birds at rest.
It seemed all the airplanes in the world had landed.

Safe thus far, we ventured to the port where
the situation seemed equally strange.
Bobbing in the waters, it seemed
all the small ships in the world had anchored.

Taking refuge in a nearby hotel
our table was arrayed with fine china and
crystal bowls holding fresh fruit, cheese, cold cuts and fresh breads.
The rich, dark intense coffee was not allowed to cool in our cups.

For the Love of Carpets

Though carpet names are lost in antiquity,
their stories are not. Their legends live on . . .
Stunning carpets everywhere, they entice learning their histories,
from their vibrant colours and designs
evoke stories of millennia.

I absolutely love carpets, I enjoy them
am in awe of them. I see their patterns,
their colours, but more than that,
I feel them; wonder how they talk
to each other. Converse through
design, texture, and colour.

I wonder about the meaning of carpets and
how they came to be?
I am drawn to carpets and their beauty.

My memories are long.
An antique carpet spotted through a window, garnet and
glowing in late afternoon sun; a cottage near Stonehenge.

I knelt on a carpet, was blessed by the Chancellor when I received my doctorate
at Cambridge. That carpet was old; timeworn silk from the hundreds who,
like me, had knelt on it for centuries.
Arabiya was a carpet oasis for me.

On evenings where there was nothing to do,
we would often look at each other and say,
"Let's go look at carpets!"

Looking at carpets
meant sitting in a room, or in rooms, piled high with carpets:

Balouche, Farahan, Hariz, Kashan, Tabriz, Isfahan, Qumm,
Na'een, Hamdan, Malaha, Caucasus and more.

Looking at carpets
meant many, many cups of mint tea.
Talking and Learning. Learning and Talking.
At session's end there would be
    a huge mound of carpets piled one on top of the other.
    More work for merchants who seemed never to tire of
    the showing and explaining, no matter how high and deep
    the piles of carpet had grown.

Carpet souqs are about the love of carpets and
the human pleasures of visiting and sharing and the telling of stories.
Evenings like these transcend ethnic boundaries and rivalries.
While our tongues loosen in talk about imminent and real war
Carpets mediate the dangers around us,
take centre stage, for a time at least,
Bring strangers together in shared comfort and human warmth.

The Day My Trees Disappeared

My shock when the few trees around our compound
in this dry land all but disappeared.

The Afghani gardener, who volunteered to trim the acacia trees
around our house, came with a question when I was home alone. "Cutting?"

The branches at the front of our place definitely needed attention;
It was getting difficult to enter the compound without being showered with
desert sand and dust. Trimming was what I had in mind.

With his saw and a big machete in hand,
this man seemed to know what he was doing.
He began; poised and seemingly in perfect control.
Before long, I heard his impatient call: "Madam."

My horror to find mere stubs on the trunks,
a great pile of branches on the ground.
The trees were naked and he was leering at me in demand for the money
he claimed I owed him. Not knowing local ways I paid what he demanded.

Violent and vulgar; there are disparities around me.
And so I seek joy in sad places. Try to lift up that which is bruised
Bring comfort to the fallen.

Gladys of Sudan

Gladys was hopeful about unification and peace in her country.
Amidst hopes for a brighter future she organized a basket-cooperative
of more than two hundred Sudanese women.

Gladys, marketing agent, loved travelling to Dubai Global Village to sell
Big baskets, small baskets, huge baskets,
woven serving trays of brilliant colour combinations. These women
know how to mix purple and red and orange and black.

We were captivated by Gladys and her stories, but
more by her visions for peace and a flourishing economy.
But there has not been peace.

So how is the women's cooperative now? Does it still flourish?
Does Gladys think of us as we remember her and
enjoy the stunning baskets we bought from her?

The friendships of global wanderers are often beautiful in their beginnings, but
transient and sad in their impossibilities—the seeming endings—without ways
to reconnect and continue what was started.

It is as Francis Bacon says that there is no excellent beauty
that hath not some strangeness in the proportion.

Carpet Repair

We met Mr. Khan on an evening when threats of war were pressing in.
Needing respite from the tensions all around
the souq gave diversion — visual, conversational, tactile, and human.

The kiosk was new. Its proprietor from Iran,
fearful too of what might happen.
In no hurry and sensitive to the conflicted emotions around us,
we stopped at the new place marked CARPET REPAIR,
where a friendly man invited us in to sit on some carpets.
We drank mint tea — an invitation to converse more deeply.

Aptitude, attitude and acquisition of skills
passed down for centuries within his lineage:
knowledge of plants and the colours they yield,
knowledge of plant properties and the methods required to
extract plant colours from blossom, leaf, stem and root;
knowledge of colour fixation techniques: the use of
animal and human urine, salt, water, and myriad other fixatives.
Knowledge too of the artist:
inspiration and creative force applied in
combinations of colour, pattern, and texture.
Knowledge of materials: hair of goat, of camel, and of sheep,
of horse and cow; and of their hides, all
receive colours in their own specific ways.
We were transfixed, but more was yet to come . . .
. . . Mr. Khan's lessons applied.

From behind a curtain he brought forth an aged rug with a large tear
and several cardboard boxes of wool samples.
How can such a large hole be mended?

Quiet settled on the shop and in ourselves as
we watched a miracle unfold before us.
Little by little—one strand and one colour at a time—
the large gap in the lovely old carpet began to disappear.
After a few hours of Mr. Khan's magic, the carpet was whole again.
It was impossible to tell where the hole had been.

We think often of Mr. Khan and his gifts, of his patience and sharing
His humanity shared amidst the tensions of
impending war bearing down upon us.

Mr. Khan left us with other gifts as well,
especially a deepening value for beauty in its myriad forms and conviction
that conflicts are best relieved through beauty and its delicate release.
There in carpet heaven we bought carpets and were gifted with carpets.
I treasure them all, each one.

The carpet I did not buy is settled in my mind.
It called to me then and calls to me still.
Sometimes I wonder if the carpet is still there waiting for me.
Woven from vegetable-dyed wool, it is in the colours of saffron and
freshly ground mustard, turmeric and indigo. In case you should visit,
it hangs just to the left of the door at Bilal's shop.
Carpets *do* matter.

Desert Kitchen

I have shopped and cooked and eaten through labyrinthine menus
Tasted unexpected foods worldwide.
I've set up kitchens in many foreign lands.
This is not easy work, patience is needed to learn new ways.
Eat local, eat well — on a shoestring.
I enjoy exploring local provender in kitchens wherever I am.

My desert kitchen is irregular and sparse.
Who could design such a kitchen?
Its triangular shape and sharp points bring unending frustrations
despite unending market ingredients fresh and often spectacular:
whole tuna caught and brought from the Gulf nearby
silvery smelts, shark and creatures too many to name.
Lamb and goat, fresh tomatoes, zataar and all manner of spices.

Fish sellers take as much pleasure as I in their offers:
"We open a new one;" that is, open a whole new tuna — for me.
Cut from a six foot tuna — I request a kilo — roughly two dollars.

From spices piled in high heaps on jute mat floors
I wanted to try cooking with all of them.
Sometimes it was hard to pay for food at the market.
Often when I asked the price, the reply was "Take 'em."
Adding to the gifts in my desert kitchen.

Language

Language.
What a wonderful thing
Even small greetings connect.

How beautiful that a few shared words
(in our own languages)
can convey friendliness and
interest in knowing more about each other.

I do my best to communicate despite
the sounds that lay so foreign and heavy on my tongue.

I stumble when I try to connect
the thoughts in my brain
with what I want to say.

I reach out and in and all around for
Language.

Perfumes & Chypres

Wonders of the ancient world

Perfume Garden

These fragments of experience.
Are they for war?
Or for peace?
Depending on perspective or conviction,
meanings blur, generate yet more questions
yield ever more combinations, their
dualities distilled in words
like scarcity or abundance;
safety or danger; pleasure or pain.

Humans cannot stand so much reality.
Flowers and perfumes are needed.
As lovely as words,
Perfumes can blend disparities,
bring mountain and plain together;
cause streams to flow in the desert.

Come now, discover an alphabet of jasmine
Write it on tablets of the heart,
Place it, carefully, in museums of the mind.

Royal Oman Symphony

Enter through a timeless passage thick with perfumes;
A strong, intense and rich curtain to find
Women laden with gold,
Men in ceremonial robes trimmed in silver,
Heads turbaned in cashmere of finest patterns and colours.

Musicians spectacularly arrayed:
women in gowns of bougainvillea in
hot colours of oranges, pinks and greens;
Their necks hung with exotic pieces.
Their heads adorned in circlets of gold with fringes of silver.
Rock crystals and rhinestones. Diamonds and pearls.

When things are grand, something happens in the human psyche;
affects relationships and landscapes. Refashions work and paradise
opens windows, stretches common humanity,
Permeates senses. Inspires stories that grow with the telling;
Translates into music and iterations of mind.

Timeless. Twists concealed now revealed. Movements.
And the moon stops to embrace a warm Omani night.

Women's World

Whisked into women's space I learn
what matters.

Inner parts of the compound
a world all its own.

First, a round of perfume, followed by
incense, strong, affronting and invasive.

Next, the scarf.
And then the clothes.

Though veils and abeyas cover the face and body,
the underneath of things tells another story.

Haute couture, colour and exquisite lingerie
Glamorous layers beneath the cloaks of black.

Like water in the felaj,
It is the underneath of things that really matter.

Spasation

Magical. Haven of wellbeing. Scented and set apart from the
rapacious construction of new hotels and their fabulous spas.
Rituals reflecting therapeutic traditions of countries nearby
There is something for everyone — for every woman that is.

In anticipation, I smell the perfume, welcome its warm embrace
like the comfort of warm waters and a panoply of stars.

The stage is set for gentle joys and gladness:
steam bath, Morocco body exfoliation, full body
massage with fragrant oil, manicures, pedicures, haircuts and more.

Mothers. Sisters. Daughters. Women in groups — whole
families of intergenerational women — babies to grandmothers and
great grandmothers. Groups of friends — visiting and gossiping,
sharing coffee and sweets in a happy world of women.

I enjoy listening to their conversations or becoming part of it.
Their talk of children and food; and
sometimes about men, and travel and dreams.

At session's end, there is a sense of rejuvenation and wellbeing.
My feet are healthy and happy to venture into the sun and hot sand.
Toenails fresh with Picasso's red, they are ready to step into my waiting
sandals, lead me expectantly into the heat of a busy or relaxing day.

Reasons for Red

Beautiful objects arranged to radiate.
Magical birds; Yeats.
His poem, Sailing to Byzantium
Re(a)d it — take it to the desert
The magic of a tomato.
The magic of painted toes.

Transcend

Every day make a triple offering of incense to the Sun, an offering of resin at sunrise,
of myrrh at midday, and of chypre at sunset.
— PLUTARCH, ISIS & OSIRIS —

Perfume transcends meanings. Treasures often hid away
Mysterious, powerful, enticing.
Though we sense different smells, we never glimpse
the scents that come to our nostrils.
Our eyes cannot perceive their fiery heat nor see their cold.

We cannot explain their wonders, their endless varieties, their sources,
the bottles designed to contain them, the trying and testing,
the gifts, the mixing and the matching nor
the stories about perfume to seduce and love;
to heal and to bind up; for tea; to sleep and to wake up.
Their makers are eager to teach and to share their stories.

Oh, the traditions of chypres. Heavy. Rich.
Some old with formulas long and complex that
Present as epic or as poetry.

Fragrances to blend past, present and future.
Use for holy days and holidays and every day;
they are beyond romance. Transcendental. Capable.
Evoking relations and nuance. They distill history,
remind us of life's symbolic elements.

Amouage

Amouage. The world's most expensive perfume.
The name of Oman's own House of Perfume.
Scents from millennia of perfumery, journeys of a different kind.
Evocative and sensory with language inspired by desert and voyage.
Sensuality—for women and for men.
Scent descriptions to lead the whole person in
surprising directions and to unexpected places.
Scents blending with other art forms
Bring ways of traveling through perfume.

Journey for Man
leaps into the unknown with spice and heat; bold and unafraid with notes of pepper, bergamot, cardamom, neroli, bigarade, juniper, gerniol, tobacco, cypriol, leather and ambrox.

Journey for Woman
an invitation to quiet, suggests paths strewn with notes of apricot, cardamom, honey, jasmine, osmanthus, saffron, nutmeg, mimosa, cedar, tobacco, vanilla, cypriol, musk and honey.

Reflection
opens with lush freshness of morning dew in the spring time. A bouquet of white flowers crowns fragrance embracing deep musks and woods wrapped with warm amber notes.

Ciel
bursts alive with the freshness of rich floral notes, leaving an inner warmth of lightness and serenity. Brings near the aura of clouds and distant sky.

Jubilation

created for the elegant and sophisticated woman who lives her life as an art form, transcending the time, place and cultures in which she inhabits.

Ubar

romances mystery and splendour as paradise is regained with echoes of bergamot and lily that complement the majestic damascene rose with the eternal presence of sandalwood.

Lyric

brings transient beauty, a poignant song without a beginning or end. Inspired by the rose, a floral fragrance suspended in time with a mythical melody.

Memoir

represents female complexity and charm through subtle cardamom notes blending mandarin orange, pink pepper and wormwood in a multidimensional and unforgettable fragrance.

Epic Woman

refers to journey, inspired by legends of the ancient Silk Road. Where desert winds blow and stars guide the search for long lost arias and a legend is born.

The Library Collection, Opus VIII

explores dialogue between illusion and reality with meticulous attention; fragrance designed to linger amidst perception and truth.

These are versions of reality defined by perceptions and perfume.
A special knowledge, this poetic homage celebrates virtuosity and truth,
reveals facets of life journey and discovery along the way.

*Perfumes are welcome in the pearly dawn of the rising sun,
at noonday and into the night to sweeten sleep and
transform one day into another.*

Sillage

Like pearls and perfume,
words are palpable and physical,
as real as stones or apricots.
Make meaning.

Like perfumes. Meanings
Shift and flow, appear and disappear
Revised. Enlarged
As invisible tracks in the air.

How does a pearl come to mean?
Or perfumes their meaning?
Shifting as veils, as messages on wind.

Like words. Real. Not fixed.
Make my mind glow.
Present as spirits to follow.

Come, they say
Present your stories from
a scent filled journey.

Honey

Manhattan of the Desert.
Yemen.
One of a kind.
Yemen.
Known for wild honey.

Steeped in legends as old as time; honey, the first thing Adam ate.
Dark and glistening like a brown night mixed with amber,
Honey from bees that gather nectar from the Sidr tree which
Grows wild in the desert. Every drop a spark of life.

Wild honey and song of the Sidr tree
Life, blossoms and the ways of bees
all life in relation with
Tree and honey and every good thing.

Like oranges and dates, this fruit is delicious
possibly good enough for dancing.

With legends of sacred rituals and
beekeepers who for thousands of years make
pilgrimage to Wadi Do'an, birthplace of Yemeni honey.

Yemen.
Where bees dance
the yellow flowers of Sidr trees
make honey that tastes of jasmine and of God.

Desert Sand

Desert sand makes me think. Tremble.
Like the strength and beauty of the sea,
or the mystery of a winter blizzard's cold white,
speaks of great forces and life changing powers.

Nature. United. Together.
Written in grandeur and terror.
The whole shakes; comes clean and
glistens in a language of perfume and ancient words.

Stop to rest, find a place with birdsong and music,
With the sweet fragrance of jasmine.
Awaken. You are not alone.
This is a place strewn
with the light of diamonds.

Aromatic Legends

Like the scents of the perfumes, their stories
merge with ancient traditions, achieve mythic qualities in the telling.
Draw inspiration from history, beauty and mystery
have their own efficacies to bind and to loose, to build up or break down,
to calm or to stimulate, to repel or to entice.

Intimate relationships their own oasis;
clefts in the many rocks of human experiences, transformed
with the blending of essence to their own effects and purposes,
understand their powers with oils enough for a thousand nights.

Even brief encounters with these perfumes suggest
they are finely crafted, highly artistic and exotic.
Steeped in timeless proverbs of survival, sensuality and gift exchange
Mindful that those who give generously shall have it returned.

The Holy Scriptures admonish that humans cannot live by bread alone;
in the Arab cultures, perfumes are also needed.

Saffron – Rose –Jasmine – Root of iris – Cumin – Bitter almond
Guaiac wood – Patchouli – Pink bay – Vanilla – Cardamom
Balsamon – Frankincense – Myrrh – Lilies – Cassia – Cedar
Sandalwood – Amber – Ouhd
Musk and many more.

Cairo Perfume Shop

I am close— very close—to levitation when
The perfume merchant introduced exquisite essences.
Explained travels to his flower farms in Alexandria, and
picking roses before dawn when their fragrance is full.
About attar and distillation, and
the powerful essence of rose that,
well-constructed, adds vital elements to the essence of other
roses like damascene rose. Helps capture fullness in bouquet
makes the heart notes exceptionally strong, lasting, and valuable.

A process to capture romantic notes
Blend alchemy and science together in a long and slow process
involves the distillation of fresh roses into sandalwood
to yield fragrance that is richer and more fragrant than its lovely base.

Attar, an essential oil from flowers,
especially the damask rose,
used pure or as a base for perfume:
attar of roses.
Attar as fire burning and unburning;
visible and invisible.
Attar as heat, as energy
Attar as fire and luminosity.

Perfume as Nature's gifts. Exquisite components for life and living
Notes for blending, they read as music, fall like poetry
infuse the mind, inspire imagination, refresh the body, mind and spirit.
Perfumes as lively forces to connect people, generate stories
transcend ideology and dispel clouds of war.

I sometimes think we can only love one another when our sense of smell
helps us make choices to which we may not otherwise surrender.
Much older than reason, the sense of smell can lead the way.
Perfumes enhance life force, restore energy that is low and feeble.
Denied so often now, scent is primal, archaic, and even mathematical;
something which can guide the eye, the body and the mind.
As a profound guide, perfume is a rich and extraordinary resource,
bids our intimate acquaintance and expanded understanding;
brings fire with luminosity to guide and satisfy life journey.

Body & Soul

Gifts of the desert

Space and Time

Vast of vast. All. All here is vast.
I am drawn into the unknown
spaces of this vast place.
Places that are at once
beyond the maps and inside them.
There is an obscurity here that attracts me,
helps make a foreign compound
a house and a home.

A home away from home.
Home is what we want. Need.
Wherever I go. Wander.
I cannot desist,
resist the remaking of
strange new places into home.

I am obsessed with hunting
and gathering
and finding things.
Found things, together.
to mix and to match or even to mix with no match
It does not matter as long as
the end reminds me of a place that is
Home.

The Other Compounds

I know there must be people in the other compounds
scattered across our part of the desert, an
outpost of the larger town.

I do not have a language, even in English, for
the geographic and political configurations here
Certainly no grasp of the local language.

What will I do here? And how will I do it?
As the morning grows hotter, I venture through the gate
Look at the world around me.
Who will I talk with in the long days ahead?
And what will we talk about?

I see a tall, thin man at the compound wall next to ours.
I watch him gather sticks and carry water. I am curious.
He too seems a stranger. Why is he here at the desert's back?
Who, besides this man, lives inside the compound?

When he disappears inside the compound gate,
my thoughts turn again to me.
How will I function in this abrasive place?
Alone from early morning until early evening
at the foot of these black mountains.

Neighbours

As one hot dry day merges into another hot dry day,
I wonder about the people living beyond the compound walls.

For brief moments when the compound gates are open,
I observe some of them, catch snatches of their routines.
At times I see them, come out and drive away or
return and disappear quickly inside the compound walls.
Sometimes I catch glimpses of the women who live inside:
graceful shapes in black with willowy movements.

But then the heavy iron gate swings shut and their lives continue
inscrutable to me. I wonder when I will meet them.

Their fleeting image is comforting. Like there might be some windows in the
walls separating me from my neighbours and the other foreigners in this
land that is so far away from my own.

Words

In many ways the desert is a blank page. Beautiful.
It invites me to think and to write,
makes me unable to stop scribbling
in my mind at least, and
sometimes on paper.

In some ways the desert is like the prairies about which
some say there is little to see.
But I love the prairie and I love the desert.
I am profoundly in love with each *and* in that order.

On the desert — in the mornings or after the wind
its surface pristine.
But soon the tracks gather.
By day's end it is reconfigured.
I like thinking from that clean surface
find shape and meaning in ancient ideas
below that surface and deep inside of me.

Spirit pours out as I find words with which to
think about this ancient land.
I add new meanings to my life
add desert gifts to my life.

Rituals of Hospitality

Arab rituals of hospitality are definite:
Water — Perfume — Food — Coffee
Each a gracious offering to honour
guests in a hot and arid land.

Water, supreme gift, for washing
Rosewater and perfumes to refresh
Choose the scent which suits you best
Partake freely of food, generously given.

Follow with coffee (*khaweh*),
flavoured with cardamom *and* rosewater,
served with dates to uplift the spirit
and remember how life is sustained.

These are the ties that bind,
synonymous with welcome and blessing;
needed for holy days and holidays and every day.
Affirmation of God's everlasting presence
Allah Baraka.

These are rituals of local histories, retraced
in gifts to refresh and sustain;
in new tastes and unexpected blends that
speak to the embeddedness of art, and
archives hidden in the chemistries of food.

These are precious offerings
of what people know;
of skills passed down for centuries,
recounted in the flow of lineage stories.

Soups and stews— vegetable, lentil, lamb and chicken
Salads from eggplant, watercress, nutmeats and spices
Vegetable curries, barbecued kebabs, grilled chicken and fish.
Aromatic breads sometimes plain, sometimes
flavoured with dates, sesame, zataar and garlic.
Ceremonies to grace with apricots, bananas and grapes.

And so we learn that it is in thinking about the specific
that we can comprehend the greater general, and
understand how simple abundance is
revealed and nurtured in rituals of hospitality.
Allah hum d'Allah.

This Morning

Early this morning

           A tree spoke to me
              Caught my attention
                Bade me listen.

As I listened

           It bade me
              Watch it move
                Bend with the wind.

As I watched

           It bade me listen
              Observe its form
                Listen to its shape.

Witness the break

           That makes it differ
              From other trees
                Crooked not straight.

Taking my breakfast

I wonder about

The meaning, the lesson

Why this tree? Why me?

Has the tree spoken before

When I did not pay heed

Did not know nor understand

The hidden life of trees?

I face my work today

Blessed and expanded

With this knowledge that

A tree blessed me.

Dance the Date

The dark-brown tree of Enki, I hold in my hand.
The tree that tells the count. Great heavens ward weapon,
I hold in my hand. The palm tree, great tree of oracles, I hold in my hand.

Dance the date. Who can live without its brown goodness,
full of itself, enabling sweetness. The desert yields it.
Its deliciousness will sustain you.
Dance the date. Embrace the hotter.
Let fruit glisten in the heat of its sun.
Refresh yourselves. [Eat]. Flesh from flesh!
Create a bone with pure, seductive pit,
with strength to sustain the human heart.

———

Blazing heat is what date palms need to thrive.
The hotter it gets, the happier they are.
In fierce temperatures they are fecund
sway seductively, transpire as their babies grow.
Glisten and bend in their gestation,
clustered loads become heavy and heavier,
fronds enrapture to soaring heat.

Young dates are like pearls,
then green like olives and
when ready, darken to sticky brown;
ooze their own delicious syrup
speak to oracles, bring satisfaction.

War Changes Things

The rhythms and rules changed drastically the morning after
the war began. A woman in an abeya approached me
confidently. Asked directly, "Do you speak English?"

Her relief was palpable to my "Yes."
Launched her into story — her words spilled out:
An émigré, she had for many years lived in America.

Anticipating re-entry, she had returned "home," to visit.
But the visit was not going well. She did not experience
acceptance by her own people.

It was Christmas season and she *wanted* Christmas.
Explained how she missed the cultural milieu now familiar and
desperate to connect, transcend lines of separation.

Home

Sometimes it's a cat that helps make a house a home.
Or stones, arranged nicely together, in the shape of
a heart—heavy and green and solid.

Sometimes a door or windows beckon
travelers to safe places, ancient and warm with
things to uplift and delight the soul.

An ancient gate perhaps opening to the future,
Release from dilapidation and desperation
offers a place where spirits can soar.

Villa al Felaj: At once a place of inspiration and solitude.
I was hemmed within the compound walls, layered and distant
from the places and people beyond.
But night brought magic all its own; sequestered and curtained
with soft light, foliage drapes and shadowed by bougainvillea lace.
Constantly evolving; a reinvention; a collection of passions and places,
of objects gathered for a tapestry from the things I found.

While some people argue about material possessions, not I;
With icons speaking of other times and other places; I
search for creative expression, and find the art of human being.

Prayer in the Time of Corona

Adhan, the Muslim call to prayer
Changeless feature of life in the Arab world
—in war and peace, in prosperity and famine—
The familiar chant echoes, five times each day.

Corona virus changes things. March 2020.

Hayya alas-salah (come to prayer) became
As-salate-fi buyutikim (pray in your homes)
Words seemingly immutable — immutable no longer.

Al-Azhar, Sunni Scholastic Centre decrees
meetings could be stopped altogether.
Egypt caps Friday sermons at 15 minutes.
Al-Aqsa Mosque, Jerusalem, is closed indefinitely.

When Saudi Arabia cancelled *umrah* pilgrimage
astounded Saudis swapped photos of the prayer plaza
deserted except for a few workers spraying disinfectant.
Decisions concerning *haj* yet to make.

In Jerusalem, the Western Wall, holiest site
Where Jews are permitted to pray
Is largely deserted, and
Rabbis urge the faithful not to kiss the stones.

Beauty is as Beauty Does

On the oasis at Wadi Bani Khalid, the winds are gentle
zephyrs in the thick warm air, redolent with
the green of palm and brown of date.

But on top of Jebel Shyams the winds are sharp and piercing,
like needles thrusting their way through the blanket;
fiendish, dervish, absolute and wild.

Remembering about being on top of that wild and open place
where one arrives at the oasis by way of a sharply gorged wadi,
the meaning of place is sensed in shallow pools of
soft green water far and sharply below.

On the other side, the Empty Quarter of the Wahiba Sands
stretches out forever, to Yemen and Saudi Arabia, and farther,
into oceans and the mysteries of the firmament.

My exploration by way of language connects to
what is vital and abundant in this part of the world, and
to making known some of that which is unknown.

It has been a journey of the heart. The spectacular beauty of
transforming my experience of a journey and ideas into
explanatory, interpretive, reaching and giving words.

Their power and efficacy connects ideas, transcends culture,
describes experience, captures emotion, and retraces history.
Despite my drawing on them they are inexhaustible, still going strong.

The transparency between this world and my language is inescapable;
a profound mystery of images and words to shape what is mysterious and
culture-laden; of what is luminous and joyous about being human.

A narrative that follows the stars and the sexton of the seas,
seeks to listen to the messages of the winds and of perfume, find meaning from
the ancient compass points available to all who choose to see and listen.

In the last half century, Arabs have created daring new societies,
reinterpreted Islamic economics, forged international identities.
How one reads their new traditions is open and invitational.

Green Parrots in my Garden is a nomadic encounter — locating through
experiences what could not be approached by research: anthropological,
religious, architectural, historical, economic, or of nutrition and cuisine.

Like perfumes it is a blend;
an alphabet of jasmine and roses,
of deserts and cities,
of camels and their riders,
of love and of war.

Guided by my senses, the journey continues,
points to wisdom from surprising sources.
Modern physics. Indeterminacy.
Dark matter and dark mass.
From life and light.

Sometimes I Remember

Sometimes I remember early mornings when
the green parrots called to me in my garden, bade me turn
my mind to my little green book. They call and
like the desert, invite me to think and to write.
Suggest fecundity — of colour and imagination. Uninhibited flow.
Miracles that rescue from inhibition.
Traversing the world and the word to arrive at new places.

Inveterate hunters and gathers. Pliers of the sea and the sand.
What is it we are seeking? Perhaps a sister in the wind?
Will we find an alphabet in jasmine or among the fish of the sea?
What museum of mind can tell, bear witness,
that search for a poet or a mother?

Knowledge waits to be mined in the fertile soil of human experience.
Waits for discovery and translation. Waits to unlock relationships
like skin, have maps of their own; reveals language, people and places.

And so, the green parrots in my garden are a universal story,
the quintessence of reality. Perceived in human language and
that of the birds and the trees . . . tells the story of the universe.
Its imprint is everywhere and in every thing.

GLOSSARY

**Since Arabic words are not standardized in English,
I have done my best to use a common spelling for words having many spellings.**

Arabiya, Arabia. Area composed of the Arabia Peninsula bounded by the Persian Gulf on the northeast, the Strait of Hormuz and the Gulf of Oman on the east, the Arabian Sea on the southeast and south, the Gulf of Aden on the south, and the Red Sea on the southwest and west; and marked at the north with the northern boundaries of Saudi Arabia and Kuwait. "There are two kinds of Arab country. On the one hand, those with a vast and living history and a social life that makes London feel cold and dead ... And on the other, those countries with the comforts and ease provided by the oil economy that you feel Year Zero was declared when the oil started flowing."(Robin Yassim-Kassab)

Alla hum d'Allah: Thank God. All praise is due to God.

Ambrox: Plant-based scent used as a base note in perfume; warm, sweet and inviting.

Areesh: Woven grass and reed used as shelter in desert building.

Bahore: Fragrances compressed into small briquettes ready to be used as incense.

Baraka: An expression of thanks and blessing.

Chokran. An expression of thanks.

Chypre: Aromatic essences made from essential oils.

Cypriol: A sweet, lingering scent from the papyrus family; used in perfume as a fixative.

Dhow: An ancient style boat, originally constructed of wood.

Eid: The two main Muslim holidays, Eid Al Adha and Eid Al Fitr.

Fallow: One of the oldest colour names in the English language; a tawny-caramel colour.

Haloum; haloumi: Soft, flavourful regional cheese.

Halwah: A regional sweet made from honey, rosewater and nuts.

Jebel; Jebal: Mountain. Mountains.

Jinns: Spirit creatures formed by God from smoke and fire.

Karam: Generosity.

Kepre: Gigantic scarab mythologized as responsible for the sun's rising and orbit.

Kohl: Eye potion originally made from soot mixed with animal fat and/or metallic minerals.

Koran: Common English spelling for the Holy Book of Islam; See Qur'an.

Labneh: Thick, cultured milk; somewhat like yogurt but thicker and tastier.

Mosque: Islamic place of worship.

N Sha'Allah: Expression and blessing reminding of God's abiding presence.

Neroli: Bitter orange flower whose deep scent is used in perfume.

Niqab: Woman's face covering.

Osmanthus: Small evergreen plant with white flowers and intense scent; used in perfume.

Shaslik: Pieces of meat, usually marinated, then barbecued on a skewer.

Sheik: Arab leader, especially head of a political unit, clan, village.

Umm: Arabic for Mother.

Wadi: A dry streambed (valley) that fills rapidly with runoff water when it rains.

Waliyat: A politico-religious region or district.

IMAGES and CREDITS

Amazing Grace. *Oasis in the Desert* by Antal Ligeti (1823-1890), Hungarian Landscape Painter who worked in the Middle East and painted in a tradition that tried to capture the natural and imagined wonders of the region.

Land & Sea. *Muttrah Fort, Oman.* I discovered David Bellamy, UK artist and author, on a generic site of desert images. Happily, I was able to locate the artist and am grateful for his permission and assistance in using his images in this book.

Sticks & Stones. *Cradles of History.* Coloured lithograph (1843) by Louis Haghe (1806-1885) after David Roberts (1796-1864). Thought to be of the ancient site of Jezreel, 9th Century BCE. Credit: Welcomme Collection; Creative Commons.

Creatures Great & Small. *Ibex.* A protected, endangered species represented for at least 6,000 years in the petro glyphs of Oman. With other regional species they contribute to mythology, science and artistry. Public Domain.

Rose & Thorn. *Bedouin Encampment*, by David Bellamy. Set against rugged desert and the need for traversing landscapes by camel, Middle Eastern lands have beauty for which modern Arabs yearn and attempt to recapture. Thank you David Bellamy.

Perfumes & Chypres. When people ask me what I miss the most about the Arab Middle East, I often say, "the perfume." Ancient traditions still lively today, but influenced by change, they bring gifts to imbue body, mind and spirit. Public domain.

Body & Soul. *Journey of the Magi.* Open Source. Images from Orientalism abound. Some present histories imagined but not real. My poems about the Arab Middle East try to reveal dynamic change: reflective of the past but actively engaged with the present and open to promise for the future.

SPECIAL THANKS

Friendships and special relationships during the Arabiya years include people from around the world: many African countries, Australia, Bangladesh, Fiji, France, India, Iran, Iraq, Lebanon, Morocco, Nepal, Palestine, Pakistan, Poland, Russia, Sri Lanka, Sultanate of Oman, Syria, UK, USA, Yemen and more.

In particular, I acknowledge Salwah and Ibrahim Ghaly who, as Middle Easterners, brought social and intellectual insights of the highest order; Mona Hauser for refuge and extraordinary imagery; Maggie and Bill Jeans for friendship, books and abode in Muscat; Dr. V. L. Shyam who introduced me to and provided Ayurveda from his clinic at Kempinski Hotel, Ajman; Marwan Elnaghi for collegiality and a special visit into Burj al Arab; Sharon and Milt Gilbertson with whom we share perspectives on Arabiya from our common home base in Camrose, Canada; Liela Abu Lughod for her evocative insights about the veiled sentiments in Bedouin culture; Peter Wheeler who graced us with his imaginative mind and his art, and Merrill Wheeler who provided important cultural insights from her work in the elementary schools at UAE and her yoga classes.

How can I ever express my delight and gratitude to the many neighbours, shop keepers, parfumers and designers from whom I learned so much.

While the green parrots visited my garden every day, it was not so easy to choose the right image for the cover of this book until I found *just* the right one in Anne-Marie Midy's book, *The Artisanal Home: Interiors and Furnishings of Casamidy*. She responded the same day I requested her permission, explaining that the green parrot image is from a hand painted tin tray in her collection. The other parrot images in this book are from open sources.

I've experienced many, many gardens with Jack Ross, my husband of five and a half decades. Creating our garden at Villa al Felaj, UAE, is amongst the best of them all. To Jack, toujours thank you — *Chokran!*

REFLECTIONS ON THE POEMS

Having lived in the UAE for 18 years, this collection revives the *magic of Arabiya* as I have known it. Jane Ross captures this magic in detail so vivid that the reader can feel the air, warmth and aromas — the *essence* — of the Middle East. Reading through the collection, I felt familiar images flash before my eyes. She even manages to portray the enchanting green (which modern Dubai/UAE definitely is) within the desert.

She touches succinctly on the culture, beliefs and values of the Middle East through parables such as *Paradise is under your mother's feet*, and creates intense visual recollections with her references to the Afghan taxi driver, the Yemeni carpet seller and the Iraqi ceramic vendor. For me, this collection is an incredible account of the Arabiya I have known during the last two decades. I love how each section starts from Jane's compound and then zooms out onto the larger UAE and Oman in a kaleidoscope of exotic Middle East ideas and images.

—**Naziha Ali,** EdD, University of Exeter, UK
Director Training, Centre for Educational Professional Development
The City School Head Office, Lahore, Pakistan. www.thecityschool.edu.pk

The joys of life in Arabiya, the highs and the lows, are all keenly crafted in Jane Ross's stunning poetry. This is a very special book, deeply affecting and nostalgic. After reading, you will dream of starlit desert nights, of the fragrance of attar, and of the beauty of a Damask rose.

A treat not to be missed and to be savoured over a glass of scented mint tea. The poetry touched my soul. What a rich, heady and exotic set of poems that linger on, long after the book is gently closed.

—**Maria Burke**, PhD MBA DMS, Professor of Management
University of Winchester, Faculty of Business, Law and Digital Technologies. London.
www.winchester.ac.uk/about-us/leadership-and-governance/staff-directory/staff-profiles/burke.php

My family has lived with parrots for over 60 years. They are amazing! *Green Parrots in my Garden* is very nice and thoughtful. The poems are good to read in times of war and peace, and even as the corona pandemic affects people in all countries. I am reading the poems in April 2020 during the corona crisis. Overall, the poems demonstrate how international experiences and even global crises bring the world together in ways that do not distinguish between rich or poor, old or young, developed or developing. Illness and death believe in equality among all people. Here in the Arab world, most people believe that corona is a curse from God as the world's sins have peaked. I hope Jane Ross keeps writing poems like these. She obviously has a hidden gift besides academics.

—**Mohsen Bagnied**, Ph.D.
University of Cairo and George Washington University, USA
Professor, Marketing and Economics. American University of Kuwait

Green Parrots in My Garden imparts an intense look into life in the Arab world from the inquisitive and open minded viewpoint of an outsider who lived there for a significant stretch of time. Jane Ross's superb collection of poems indulges the senses through description so vibrant one smells the jasmine that scented the yard of her living quarters, feels the bite of sand blown on her face during a walk in the desert and marvels at the skill of a craftsman whose artful mending restores a woven carpet to its original state. Ross deftly portrays her experiences in these faraway lands as armed conflict edged uncomfortably close. Many thanks to her for sharing her Arabiya.

—**Cathie Bartlett,** BA Honours, Western University
Battle River Writing Centre, Camrose, Alberta, Canada
Journalist and Author: Destination Prairie

"Memory fades, must the remembered perishing be?" The answer to Walter de la Mare's question in these poems by Jane Ross is a resounding "No!" In them, she relives, two decades later, the experience of "life in this strange and foreign land" (Arabiya), as if it were yesterday. The poems recall places visited: Musandam (Norway of the East), Nizwa, Jumeirah, the Hajar Mountains, the Empty Quarter, wadis, oases, Bastakiya and the Blue Souk in Sharjah; encounters with people, a carpet dealer, a parfumier, gardeners, garbage collectors, women among women. Also, and most evocatively, the poems summon up the assault on the senses in Arabiya, the fragrance of amouage and jasmine, the taste of rose flavoured coffee and Bedouin tea, the colours of bougainvillea and parrots, blazing heat, the cool of night. Vividly descriptive, the poems are also profoundly reflective, on tradition and modernity, alienation, the imminence of the Iraq War and finally the Corona catastrophe.

—**Peter J. H. Wheeler**, Artist
Professor Emeritus, Loughborough University; Le Midi, France
Dean (2000-2005), College of Fine Arts, University of Sharjah, United Arab Emirates

In her new book of poetry, *Green Parrots in My Garden*, Alberta storyteller Jane Ross brings us a compilation of enchanted verses that she wrote while living in the United Arab Emirates and the Sultanate of Oman, her home away from home on the Persian Gulf. Some are tales of caution, but mostly her poems reflect the magical zen moments she experienced while living in this fascinating area, including the city of Dubai. Green Parrots in My Garden is a refreshing book of poems; a much needed escape from these strange times in which we now live.

—**Kate Rittner Werkman,** Journalism
Arts and Cultural Management, McEwan University
Writers' Guild of Alberta, Edmonton, Alberta

I thoroughly enjoyed reading *Green Parrots in My Garden*, a collection of poems about Arabiya — a region of my own experience. Jane has a lovely writing style that is as rich and exotic as the places and people she writes about. Although scholarly and well researched, her writing never comes across as elitist. While accessible and welcoming, it also nudges one into new territory. Some of the poems are like fireworks; colourful, celebratory, and an explosion of ideas. Other poems are like the gentle, refreshing breeze of a desert oasis. For both the seasoned traveler and the traveller at heart, these poems are for me like a trip down memory lane, evoking images, sounds and smells long forgotten. The pages become dunes as Jane's artistic writing flows over them like perfume and the sands of time.

—**Lawrence Dombro**, BSc, LLB, MBA, MDP, SYT
CEO, HeartSmart Foods
Edmonton, Alberta, Canada

Through descriptions and reflection, Jane Ross invites the reader within spaces and feelings she attempts to make and keep familiar. She shares memories, aware of their worth and their transformative potential for herself — sharing as a way to remain faithful to experiences and encounters — and for those who take the time to sit with her. She avoids observations as she firmly places herself within the images she crafts in order to render moments better. This book illustrates the deep conscience of her place in the Middle East, neither only or entirely traveller nor foreigner; a pilgrim whose destination is in interactions, cities, and landscapes. Her book also often made me hungry, perhaps out of my own fondness for coffee and dates!

—**Jérôme Melançon**, PhD
Associate Professor French and Francophone Intercultural Studies; University of Regina
Author of De perdre tes pas and Quelques pas quelque part.

I am honoured to be part of this poetic journey by Jane Ross whose work in words parallels my own, albeit in a different medium. The content of *Green Parrots in My Garden*, like my visual artwork, derives from different practice chronologies to open conversations about life journeys.

I'm also delighted that Jane has chosen my mixed media work *Ode to the Emirates* — rendered on an original UAE map — to open and situate her poems. Poems, like maps, are not just two-dimensional works on paper, but documents containing untold stories of adventure, promise, memory and hope. Aesthetically they are beautiful in their own right, they act as a base for reconstructed, dissected and reimagined narratives where experiences, roads and journeys intertwine. Their practicality recalls the unattained discoveries and potential along life's ways. Like arteries, they can help relieve isolation in location and lead to new horizons.

As the map — or a life of experience — is deconstructed and reconstructed into the poems of this volume, the imagery depicted becomes more or less identifiable to the original components in their realistic and symbolic spread across the pages to become literature and ultimately encompass the whole volume. Jane's writing reveals her respect for the people she has met. The care she has taken with her Middle East source materials enables me to understand how her journals have come alive through the use of thoughtful words and images evoked for moments or laid down in memories for long periods to come. By collecting and presenting fragments from her experiences, Jane's poems enable others to make journeys of the mind through time and convey meanings of a special place and period of time.

—**Naz Sharokh** (Iran), BFA, MFA, MS,
Pratt Institute, Brooklyn, NY
Visual Artist and Professor
Zayed University, United Arab Emirates

Other titles by Jane Ross

Through the Looking Glass: Children and Health Promotion
(1990). Anthology: Jane Ross and Vangie Bergum

Quality Culture: Quality for Turbulent Times.
(1994). Jane Ross, Jack Ross, Robert Hoogstoel, Lisa Anderson

Beauty Everyday: Stories from Life as it Happens
(2016). Anthology: Jane Ross, Editor

Poems from Life as it Happens
(2019). Anthology: Jane Ross, Editor

my Arabiya: Journey into the New Millennium
(2021). Jane Ross

Arts that Flow as Stories from Our Landscape: Alberta
(2021). Anthology: Jane Ross, Editor

ABOUT THE TYPE

Green Parrots in My Garden is set in Calibri, a modern typeface designed by Luc(as) deGroot. Calibri features subtly rounded stems and corners with a true italic form having handwriting influences. The typeface includes characters from Latin, Greek and Cyrillic scripts. Calibri's many curves and scalability team up to reveal a warm and soft character suitable for the nuances of the ideas and emotions of poetry and landscape.

DeGroot was born in the Netherlands where he studied at the Royal Academy of Arts in The Hague. He believes type design should be a mixture of intuition and calculation to produce text that looks healthy and friendly. His work includes custom-designed font families for numerous clients from agriculture to international sectors. He teaches in the University of Applied Sciences, Potsdam, near Berlin. His aim is to make the world better by designing typefaces that look pleasant and work well under any circumstances and in as many languages as possible.